Author:
Peter Hicks studied history at the
University of London, Open University and
the University of Sussex and is a certified
field archaeologist. He has written many
historical books for children.

Series creator:
David Salariya was born in Dundee,
Scotland. He has illustrated a wide range of
books and has created and designed many
new series for publishers both in the UK and
overseas. In 1989 he established The Salariya
Book Company. He lives in Brighton with his
wife, the illustrator Shirley Willis, and their
son Jonathan.

Artists:
Mark Bergin studied at Eastbourne
College of Art and has specialised in
historical reconstructions since 1983. He
lives in Bexhill-on-Sea with his wife and
three children.

John James was born in London in 1959.
He studied at Eastbourne College of Art and
has since illustrated many non-fiction books
for children, particulary on historical topics.
He lives in Sussex with his wife and children.

Additional artists:
Nick Hewetson
Gerald Wood

Created, designed and produced by
The Salariya Book Company Ltd
25 Marlborough Place,
Brighton BN1 1UB
Please visit us at:
www.salariya.com
www.book-house.co.uk

Published in Great Britain in 2002 by Hodder Wayland,
an imprint of Hodder Children's Books

A catalogue record for this book is available from
the British Library.

ISBN 0 7502 3582 9

Hodder Children's Books
A division of Hodder Headline Limited
338 Euston Road, London NW1 3BH

Printed and bound in Belgium.

Printed on paper from sustainable forests.

Editors:
Karen Barker Smith
Stephanie Cole

GODS & GODDESSES

IN THE DAILY LIFE OF THE

ANCIENT ROMANS

Written by Peter Hicks
Illustrated by Mark Bergin and John James

Hodder
Wayland

an imprint of Hodder Children's Books

CONTENTS

INTRODUCTION

Daily life for the majority of ordinary people living in the ancient Roman Empire was a great struggle. Many unexpected and unpleasant events could create great suffering. Crops could fail causing famine, war could break out and destroy the land, earthquakes could flatten towns and cities, sickness and disease could strike easily and death was never far away.

Not surprisingly, the gods played an important part in the lives of the ancient Roman citizens, not only as protectors against these uncertainties and tragedies, but also because they were responsible for everything that happened on the earth, in the sea and in the sky. If disasters occurred, the people feared that the gods were angry. Perhaps they had been neglected and their temples not looked after or perhaps religious ceremonies had not been carried out properly. Augustus, the first Emperor of the Roman Empire, certainly believed this and he was sure that correct worship of the gods would bring peace and prosperity. In this book we shall see how important the Roman gods and goddesses were to the everyday lives of the Roman people.

THE GODS
HISTORY AND THE STATE RELIGION

By 100 BC, Rome (below), with its one million inhabitants, was the biggest city in the world. The huge track, the *Circus Maximus*, was home to chariot racing and above it towered the temple of Apollo. Note the arches of one of the aqueducts that brought millions of litres of clean water into the city every day.

The Romans believed in many different gods and as their Empire increased in size, the varieties of religious worship also grew. In fact, their most important gods were borrowed from the Greek Pantheon and given Roman names. They had a state religion, in which the Emperor (thought of as a god) and the three most important gods and goddesses, Jupiter, Juno and Minerva, were worshipped. As long as people recognised this system, they could also worship any of the other gods.

Most towns and cities had gods or goddesses who acted as guardians or protectors and made their homes there. This silver statue of a city guardian (above) has seven busts above her wings, which represent the days of the week.

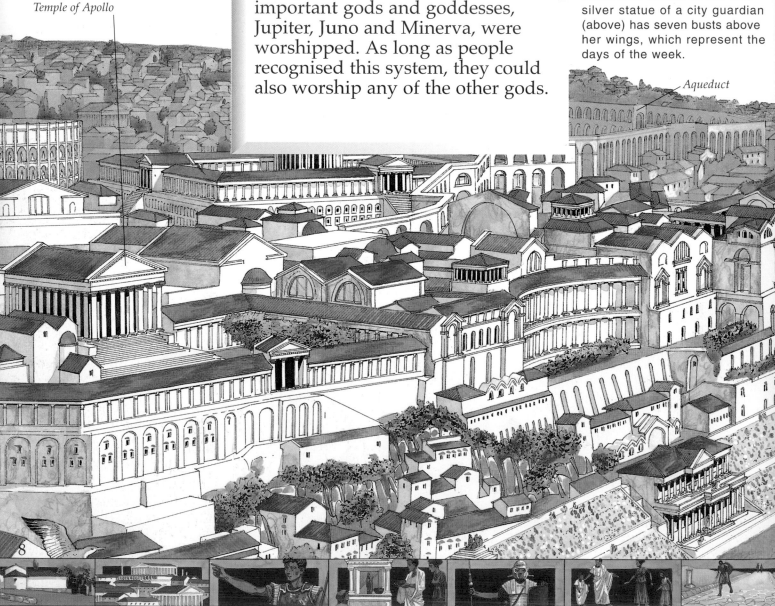

Temple of Apollo

Aqueduct

INSIDE STORY

The legendary founder of Rome is Romulus. He and his twin brother Remus were thrown into the River Tiber when they were babies. A she-wolf suckled them and saved the pair from starvation (right). A shepherd, Faustulus, and his kind wife found them and brought them up. Later, the brothers laid out a plan for the city, but Romulus killed his brother in a quarrel over who should be king. This is said to have happened in 753 BC.

Romulus and Remus being suckled by the she-wolf

Rome was built on seven hills on the east bank of the River Tiber (right). From early times temples were built to all of the important gods and the 'Via Sacra', or 'Sacred Way' served many of these. Walls surrounded the city.

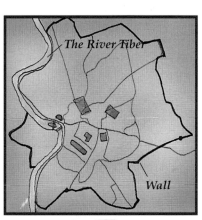

The River Tiber

Wall

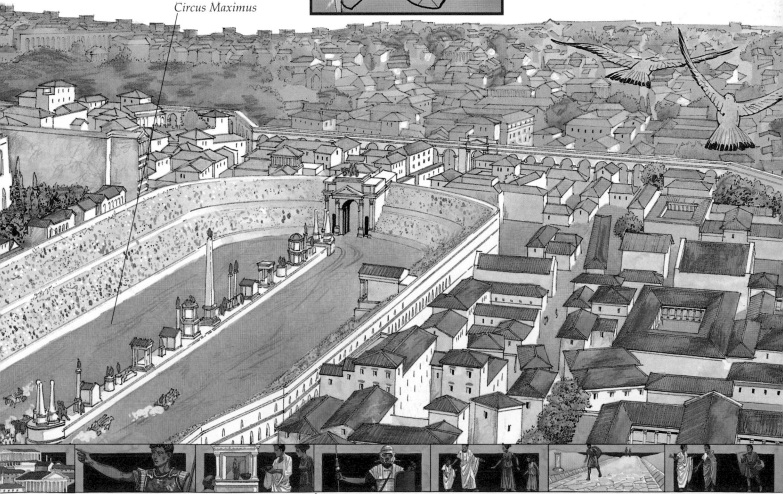

Circus Maximus

Augustus (above) fought many battles at home and abroad and was always victorious. His navy cleared the seas of pirates and made them safe for Roman trading ships. His qualities were 'goodness, victory, discipline and luck'.

Augustus, who ruled Rome from 27 BC to AD 14, was the first of a long line of emperors to be made a god after death. This was done to strengthen the power and position of the emperors at a time when the Roman Empire was growing rapidly. It often impressed the inhabitants of new and conquered provinces that the Roman emperor sat with the gods! When the emperor's body was cremated on a large funeral fire, an eagle was released. This was said to take the emperor's soul from earth to heaven.

Julius Caesar (above) was the great-uncle of Augustus and adopted him as his son. Caesar, one of the great Roman generals and leaders, was famously assassinated in 44 BC. He was also made into a god after his death.

Augustus distributed a corn dole, or ration, every month. This was five measures of corn, enough to feed one man but not his whole family. In this way Augustus became popular with the Roman citizens. This mosaic (below), found in Ostia, Italy, shows a man measuring out the corn dole.

As Commander-in-Chief of the army, the emperor was loyally supported. This altar (right), found in a Roman fort, was dedicated to the 'discipline (strength) of the emperor'.

INSIDE STORY

Vespasian was one of the twenty emperors to become a god. Originally a talented general, he was responsible for many victories, including the successful invasion of Britain in AD 43 under Claudius. He was Emperor for ten years and was a firm leader who strengthened Rome. During his final illness and in great pain, he knew he was dying. 'Oh dear', he said, 'I think I am becoming a god!'

A TEMPLE DEDICATED TO THE EMPEROR

This temple (below), dedicated to Augustus, has its altar outside the building in front of the steps. It was here that sacrifices were made, usually by slaughtering an animal. The steps lead to the platform or podium on which the temple is built.

Huge columns form a colonnade around the temple which protects people from the sun and rain. Inside is the *cella*, the special room with a shrine to the god, usually a statue and another altar for burning incense. Behind the *cella* are small rooms used by the priests and for storing treasures not on display.

Cella

Colonnade

Podium

Altar

JUPITER
KING OF THE GODS: PROTECTOR OF THE PEOPLE

This impressive mosaic (below), found on the floor of a large villa at Lullingstone in England, tells a famous story. Jupiter, disguised as a bull, carried away the beautiful Europa to the island of Crete. There, she had three sons, including Minos, who became king and built the wonderful palace of Knossos, home to the Minotaur and his labyrinth.

Probably the most important Roman god, Jupiter was known as *Optimus Maximus* – the best and the greatest. Controller of the sky, thunder, lightning and rain, he was above all seen as successful and therefore popular. 'Jupiter makes us healthy and rich and prosperous,' wrote Cicero, a famous Roman writer. Jupiter was married to Juno and a huge temple was built to them (along with Minerva) on Capitol Hill in Rome. These three were known as the 'Capitoline Triad'.

As a sky god, Jupiter used lightning bolts as his weapons (above). The ground where they landed was believed to be holy because Jupiter had claimed it for himself.

Europa

Jupiter disguised as a bull

INSIDE STORY
An important part of Jupiter's armoury was the *Aegis*. This appears in different forms – sometimes a shield, at other times a breastplate. At its most dramatic it can be seen as a thundercloud. Whatever form it took, its job was to protect Jupiter from any enemy. When he shook it, a huge thunderstorm occurred, often frightening away many of his foes!

The eagle, the strongest and one of the largest birds of prey, was often used to portray Jupiter. It was said that Jupiter himself sometimes took the form of an eagle. This Roman mosaic from Tunisia (right) illustrates the story of how when the gods wanted a cup-bearer, Jupiter swooped down on Ganymedes, a young Trojan prince, and carried him off to Olympus. Because the eagle is so powerful, the Roman army used *aquilae* – eagle standards carried by each legion – as a symbol of their strength.

Jupiter as an eagle

Ganymedes

Altar

Sacrificial bull

Procession of priests

SACRIFICES FOR JUPITER

One of the most popular events in Rome was a ceremony performed on 1st January. Large crowds assembled next to the Sacred Way to watch a solemn procession make its way to the Capitol Hill. At its head were bulls to be sacrificed to Jupiter in order that Rome be protected for another year. Fresh vows were made to him – because he was special to Rome – as the axes came down to slaughter the bulls.

JUNO
GODDESS OF CHILDBIRTH: MARRIAGE AND CHILDREN

FAMILY
Father Saturn
Husband Jupiter
Sons Mars, Vulcan

Women were very involved in matters of health and medicine. Many acted as midwives (*obstetrix*) to help women give birth and nurses (*nutrix*) to help the sick, although very few became doctors (*medici*). There were many remedies for sickness that were handed down through the ages and these would have been prepared in chemist's shops, known as *pharmacopia*. The stone relief below shows a woman seated in a chemist's shop.

Juno, the wife of Jupiter, was an immensely important goddess, especially for women. She was seen as a mother-figure and helped them in their daily lives, be it in health, marriage, fertility, childbirth or bringing up children. All these events were difficult and some often dangerous, so prayers, offerings and sacrifices were necessary if the assistance of Juno was needed. She was honoured by having one of the summer months named after her. This is where the name of the month June comes from.

This mask (above), from Hungary, portrays Juno. She was worshipped especially on the 1st March during the *Matronalia* or Motherhood festival. It was traditional for husbands to give presents to their wives and for female slaves to be feasted by their mistresses on this day.

Juno (above) was distrustful of her husband Jupiter who she thought had an eye for other women. She often sent spies to see what he was up to.

INSIDE STORY
Juno had noticed that Jupiter was interested in the beautiful priestess Io, so she sent Argus to spy on him. Argus was well qualified, as he had 100 eyes! Jupiter knew about this and he sent Mercury, the god of trickery, to kill him. This he did, and then he decided to put all Argus' one hundred eyes in the tail of the peacock (left).

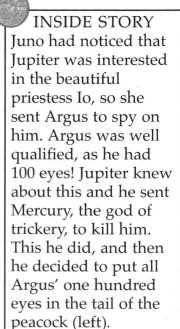

MARRIAGE

A woman always consulted Juno when she considered getting married. On the wedding day, certain rituals and customs were essential to the marriage's success. Returning home from the ceremony, jokes were shouted and nuts thrown by the guests at the couple. The bridegroom carried his bride over the threshold so she could not stumble. To have fallen would have been bad luck for the future of their marriage.

A bride and groom exchange their wedding vows (above). After the ceremony the couple would return to the husband's home for a sacrifice and a feast.

Childbirth was extremely dangerous in Roman times. Difficult births and the risk of infection were common problems. Juno was always called upon to help with both childbirth and childcare. This relief carving (right) shows a mother bathing her baby with the help of her slave.

Mother *Slave*

GODDESS OF WISDOM: CRAFTSMANSHIP AND THE ARTS

FAMILY
Father Jupiter
Brothers Apollo,
 Bacchus, Mercury
Sister Diana

INSIDE STORY
Minerva helped the hero Perseus when he fought with the gorgon Medusa, a monster with snakes for hair who could turn people into stone by looking at them. Minerva gave Perseus a shield which reflected the gaze of Medusa. This enabled him to kill her. After Medusa's head was cut off, her face appeared on Minerva's cloak.

Minerva was the talented and wise goddess of the arts and crafts. The owl became her symbol as it represented wisdom. She invented the bridle, yoke, plough and rake as well as clay pots, and for musicians she created the flute and the trumpet. For this reason, she was adopted as patron goddess by many craftsmen. They organised themselves into groups called guilds and prayed to her for prosperity. Musicians gathered at her temple on 13th June to pay her homage and to celebrate.

Minerva (above) had an extraordinary birth. Jupiter complained of a terrible headache and asked Vulcan, god of fire, to split his head open. Out leapt Minerva, fully armed with helmet and shield, as shown in this 17th-century statue. Because of this she was also known as the goddess of war.

A potter at work

Because of her connection with pottery, Minerva was highly regarded by the potters' guilds. Pottery was an important trade, for all homes needed bowls, jars and pots. This is Samian ware (above) – a fine, smooth, red tableware produced in southern Gaul (France) and moulded with attractive designs. Left, a potter is busy at work producing storage jars and jugs.

Potter's workshop

Butcher's shop

Street fountain

Wine shop

CRAFT SHOPS

In Roman towns single-unit shops were very common and opened out onto the streets from houses or apartment blocks. Some had workshops and storage areas upstairs where goods were made. Shops that were deliberately built together formed markets called *macella*. These attracted other shops and were built near the *forum*.

Mercury was a popular god because of his trickery and cunning. Incredibly fast in his winged hat and sandals, as shown on this Roman bronze statue (above), he made an excellent messenger for the gods.

Mercury was the many-talented god of trade, commerce, theft, communication and travel. Another of his jobs was to escort the souls of the dead down to the underworld. He was also protector of the corn-trade – very important because of the need to feed a large Empire – which made him popular with merchants. His festival day was 15th May and merchants and traders duly honoured their protector with processions and offerings.

FAMILY
Father Jupiter
Brothers Apollo, Bacchus
Sisters Diana, Minerva

Mercury was also known as the protector of travellers. The Roman Empire had an excellent network of roads and they were widely used. Offerings, prayers and sacrifices were made for a safe journey, because they were often risky. Brigands or highwaymen frequently robbed, beat or killed travellers on lonely stretches of road. The vehicle in this carving (below), taken from a Roman sarcophagus, was used for transporting passengers.

INSIDE STORY
From the moment he was born, Mercury had a reputation for theft. He left his cave and saw Apollo tending to his cattle. Waiting for him to fall asleep, Mercury then stole the whole herd! He led them out of the field backwards, making them walk in their own footprints so they could not be tracked. By appealing to Jupiter, Apollo got most of his herd back and a lyre (made by Mercury) for his troubles.

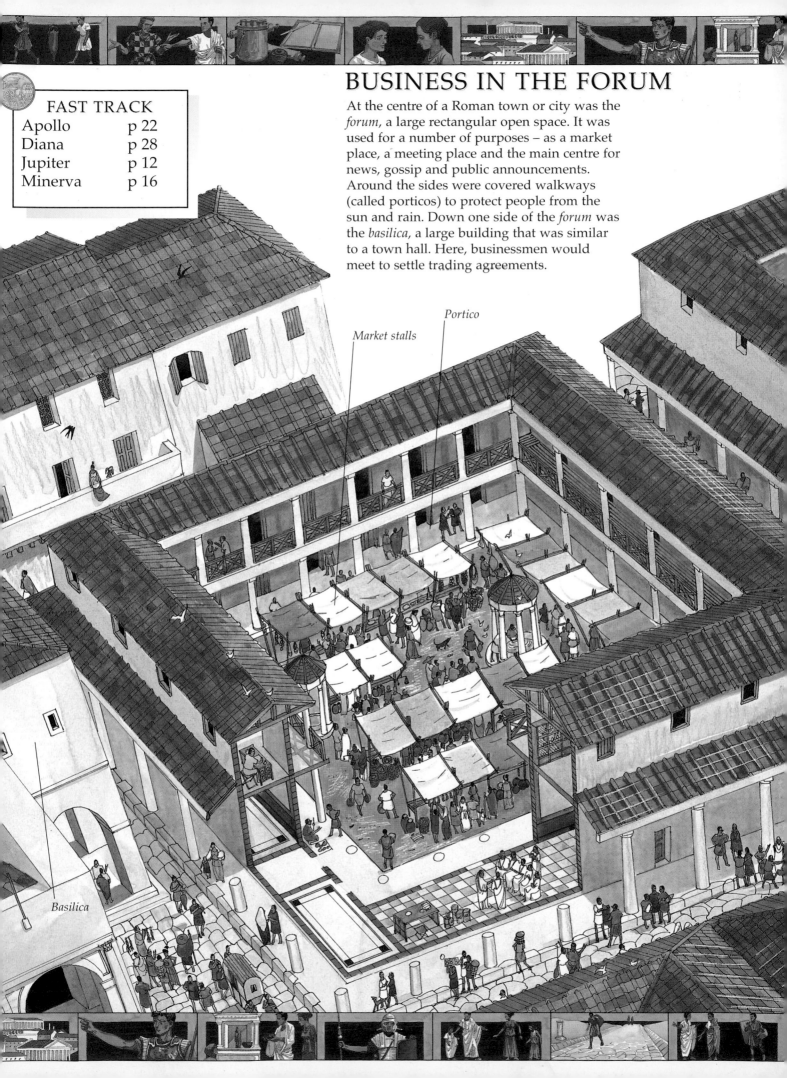

BUSINESS IN THE FORUM

At the centre of a Roman town or city was the *forum*, a large rectangular open space. It was used for a number of purposes – as a market place, a meeting place and the main centre for news, gossip and public announcements. Around the sides were covered walkways (called porticos) to protect people from the sun and rain. Down one side of the *forum* was the *basilica*, a large building that was similar to a town hall. Here, businessmen would meet to settle trading agreements.

Portico

Market stalls

Basilica

CERES

GODDESS OF CORN: FOOD AND FARMING

The main industry of the Roman Empire was farming. As the Empire grew and its population increased, a regular food supply was essential. Huge numbers of people – mainly slaves – worked on the land. Ceres, the goddess of the earth and corn, was closely involved with this food production. Getting the harvest in safely was always a hazardous affair and the power of Ceres was called on especially at this time, during the months of May, June and July.

This 4th-century-BC marble statue (above) is of Ceres. Sacrifices were made to her at the time of harvest – singing and praying to Ceres, farmers formed a magic circle to protect their harvest.

Where estates and fields met, neighbouring families gathered to honour Terminus, the god of boundaries (below). He had two heads, each of which looked towards one of the two villas, and the families offered him milk, honey and wine.

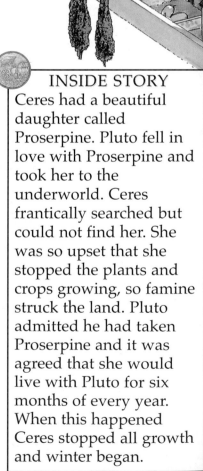

INSIDE STORY

Ceres had a beautiful daughter called Proserpine. Pluto fell in love with Proserpine and took her to the underworld. Ceres frantically searched but could not find her. She was so upset that she stopped the plants and crops growing, so famine struck the land. Pluto admitted he had taken Proserpine and it was agreed that she would live with Pluto for six months of every year. When this happened Ceres stopped all growth and winter began.

THE FARM VILLA

The centre of a farm estate was the villa. A villa consisted of a large house for the owner and his family, and all the out-buildings that were used in farm production. Large farms owned dozens of slaves to do the work. As the farm became more prosperous, the size of the villa grew. New ranges of rooms served by corridors, and even luxurious bath houses, were added. Many villas were built near to the Roman road system so produce could be taken to market easily.

FAMILY

Father Saturn
Sisters Juno, Vesta
Brothers Jupiter, Neptune, Pluto
Daughter Proserpine

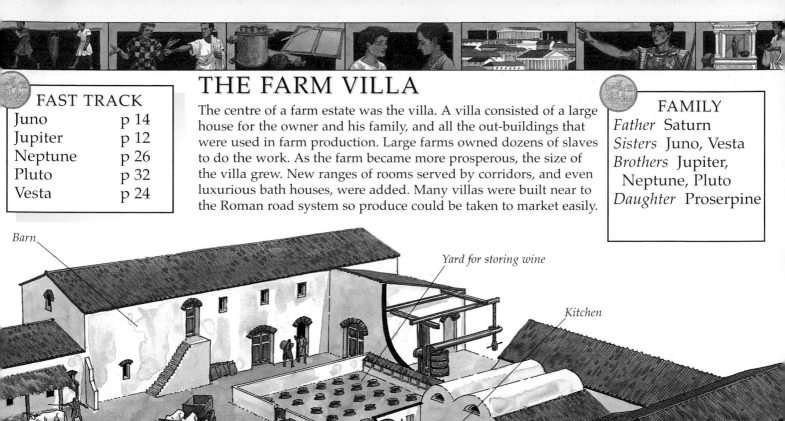

Barn

Yard for storing wine

Kitchen

Baking oven

Temple

The main crop of a villa was corn and this had to be threshed and stored before being sent to market. Other crops included olives and grapes for wine which was fermented in huge jars sunk into the ground. Animals were kept for meat and their hides, as well as for transport.

Garden

21

GOD OF HEALING: HEALTH AND MEDICINE

This mosaic (above) from the 2nd century BC shows Apollo as the sun god. Apollo was honoured by the Games in Rome during July and his festival took place on 23rd September.

INSIDE STORY

When people wanted to know the future they would often go to a place called an Oracle to ask the gods. The Oracle at Delphi in Greece was the most special because Apollo was its master. Apollo had killed a beast there, the Python – a large snake – with his silver bow and golden arrows. The priestess, the Pythia, as she was known, spoke the wisdom of Apollo and was visited by people from all over the Roman Empire.

Apollo was very highly admired. He had many talents and was skilled in music, archery, medicine, the care of flocks and herds and, very importantly, prophecy. He was a healing god and many springs, temples and sanctuaries were dedicated to him in the hope that they would bring health and cure sickness. He was also linked with the sun and its health-giving properties. A temple in Gaul (France) was dedicated to Apollo's 'clear light' and helped people suffering from eyesight problems.

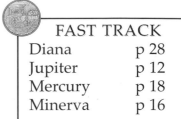

FAMILY
Father Jupiter
Mother Latona
Brothers Bacchus, Mercury
Sisters Diana, Minerva

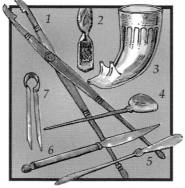

At a time when medical knowledge was limited, a god who was thought to have the power of healing was highly regarded. The items pictured above are:
1) forceps; 2) probe;
3) glass dropper for eye treatment; 4) and 5) bronze spatulas; 6) knife;
7) bronze tweezers.

Apollo was also the god of culture and creativity. He was a fine musician and was honoured by people working in the theatre. Theatres could be found in cities all round the Empire and their plays were very popular. This is the ruin of the Odeon (below) at Pompeii which was used for meetings, poetry and musical recitals.

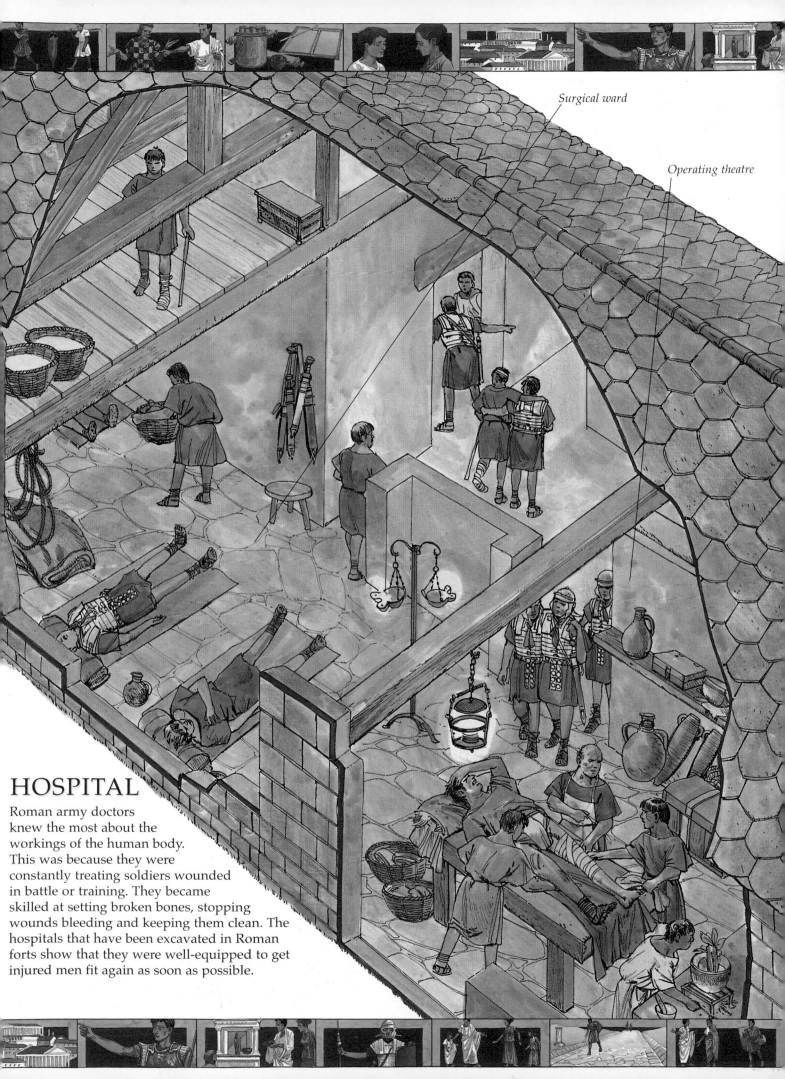

Surgical ward

Operating theatre

HOSPITAL

Roman army doctors knew the most about the workings of the human body. This was because they were constantly treating soldiers wounded in battle or training. They became skilled at setting broken bones, stopping wounds bleeding and keeping them clean. The hospitals that have been excavated in Roman forts show that they were well-equipped to get injured men fit again as soon as possible.

VESTA

GODDESS OF THE HEARTH: THE HOME

This Roman statue shows Vesta (above). During meals, families would throw a cake into the hearth as a mark of respect to Vesta. If it crackled it meant they would have good luck.

Vesta was the goddess of the home and the hearth (fireplace). She protected the house and the family and was always there to offer comfort in a cruel and uncertain world. Like the fire, she spread warmth and light. Vestalia – the festival honouring Vesta – took place on 9th June and was also celebrated as a bakers' holiday. This was because at one time all Roman families baked their own bread at the hearth.

Other important household gods were the Lares, who were the spirits of dead ancestors. They were worshipped at a *lararium* (above) where offerings like food flowers and wine were placed.

INSIDE STORY

Vesta was worshipped at a temple containing a fire thought to have been brought from Troy, in present day Turkey. It was never allowed to go out. This precious fire was looked after by six Vestal Virgins who served under a High Priest for 30 years. The fire was so sacred that when any citizen left Rome to set up a new home, he would take coals from the temple hearth. When he reached his destination these coals were used to light the first fire.

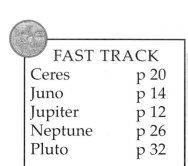

FAST TRACK	
Ceres	p 20
Juno	p 14
Jupiter	p 12
Neptune	p 26
Pluto	p 32

The keepers of the sacred flame in Vesta's temple were highly respected women. This relief carving (left) shows them at a state sacrifice. Vesta's temple was full of treasures and guarded closely. The Vestal Virgins themselves were treated well, but the penalty for loss of virginity was savage. In the reign of Emperor Domitian two Vestals were buried alive!

The kitchen was one of the most important rooms in a Roman house or villa (left). Meat, poultry, grain, vegetables and olive oil were always available there.

Reconstruction of a Roman kitchen

Atrium

Portico

Kitchen

Bedroom

Peristyle garden

Dining room

ROMAN HOUSES

Wealthy Romans lived in splendid town houses (above) that were built around a hall called an *atrium*. The house was an enclosure with few windows in the outer walls for security and to cut out the noise, dirt and smells from the street. Light came from the centre of the house where there was often a peristyle garden, surrounded by a portico. The vast majority of people, however, lived in blocks of flats. Accommodation for them was basic and often cold, dark and cramped.

NEPTUNE

GOD OF THE SEA: SHIPS AND SEAFARING

Neptune (above) was originally an ancient Italian god of water. However, he became identified with the Greek god Poseidon, who ruled the oceans. Neptunalia, his festival on 23rd July, was one of the oldest festivals in Rome.

Neptune had control over the forces of nature. He ruled the oceans and could send violent earthquakes at any time – he was known as the 'shaker of the earth'. It is less well known that he was also the god of horses – it was thought that he was the first to tame a horse so that it could help people with farming and transport. Neptune was easily recognised as he carried a three-pronged trident with him. He travelled the oceans on a dolphin or a sea horse.

Amphorae (above) were often used to store solid foods, such as dates, oysters, nuts and figs, as well as wine. They were very useful storage jars and their remains have been excavated in many houses and villas.

FAMILY
Father Saturn
Brother Pluto
Sisters Ceres, Juno, Vesta
Wife Amphitrite

This plate with Neptune at its centre (left) was found in a field in Suffolk, England.

INSIDE STORY
When the gods were young they split parts of the world up between them. Neptune did badly in the arguments over land and ended up only ruling the island of Atlantis. However, he disliked his possession and ripped the island apart with a terrible earthquake that sent it to the bottom of the sea. The Atlantic Ocean got its name from this event.

This wall mosaic (right), found in a house in Herculaneum, Italy, shows Neptune with his wife Amphitrite. After the volcano Vesuvius erupted in nearby Pompeii in AD 79, Herculaneum was completely covered by a scalding hot mud-slide which soon turned to solid rock.

SEA PORTS

Sea trade was very important for the prosperity of the Roman Empire. Transporting goods in bulk by ship throughout the Mediterranean (and beyond) brought wealth to both merchants and cities. Ostia, the port that served Rome, attracted traders from all over the known world.

10 million sacks of grain a year passed through the port to the hungry mouths of Rome! Other goods such as olive oil, wine and *garum* (fish paste) were transported in *amphorae*. The pointed ends of these containers helped with pouring and enabled them to be stacked in the holds of ships.

GODDESS OF THE HUNT: COUNTRY SPORTS

Diana was concerned with the rights of vulnerable people. Her temple in Rome was a refuge for runaway slaves. The 13th August – Diana's festival – was a special day for slaves because their owners had to give them the day off. Many of them went to the public baths (above) and enjoyed the pleasures they could only watch when attending their owners.

Diana, one of the most beautiful goddesses, had several different roles. These included helping women in childbirth and protecting children and other vulnerable people. Because of this, Diana was sometimes known as 'Juno Lucina', meaning 'she who makes children see the light of day'. As sister of the sun god, Apollo, Diana was goddess of the moon and she reflected the light from him. However, she is most famous as the goddess of the hunt and country sports.

INSIDE STORY

Despite her concern for the weak, Diana was capable of great cruelty. One day, while she was bathing in a woodland pool, the great hunter Actaeon spied on her. He was so amazed at her beauty that he moved nearer, snapping a twig and betraying his crime. Diana was so annoyed that she changed Actaeon into a stag so that his hunting dogs, not realising he was their master, ripped him limb from limb!

Hunting (left) was very popular during Roman times, for a number of reasons. It was a social gathering for friends, a way of obtaining food and a means of military training.

It was obviously not possible to hunt in the city of Rome. However, hunting was so popular with the Roman people that wild beasts were brought to Rome from hundreds of miles away. They were then taken to the Colosseum, where they were let loose to be chased by gladiators in front of huge audiences. These wild beast shows (left) were very cruel and thousands of animals were killed. Some species even became extinct in Roman lands.

THE HUNT

Hunting was a very important countryside activity for all classes in the Roman Empire. For the poor, it provided an essential supplement to a meagre diet and meat was always a welcome addition to the cooking pot. For the rich, hunting was more a mark of social status, as well as a social occasion. It was an expensive pastime. As well as the basic weapons such as spears, bows and arrows, hunters also needed nets and snares to actually catch the animals. Mosaics show that most hunts used hunting dogs that were specially bred and trained.

Geese, ducks and smaller birds were trapped in nets, while deer, wild boar and foxes were hunted on both foot and horseback. Rich Romans owned horses exclusively used for hunting. Snares were used to trap or slow down animals, while the dogs proved very effective at catching hares. For the huntsmen, food and drink and the company of their fellow hunters made for an enjoyable time. After a successful day's hunting, a sacrifice – usually one of the captured animals – was offered to Diana, goddess of the hunt.

FAST TRACK

Apollo	p 22
Jupiter	p 12
Minerva	p 16

FAMILY

Father Jupiter
Mother Latona
Brothers Apollo, Bacchus, Mercury
Sister Minerva

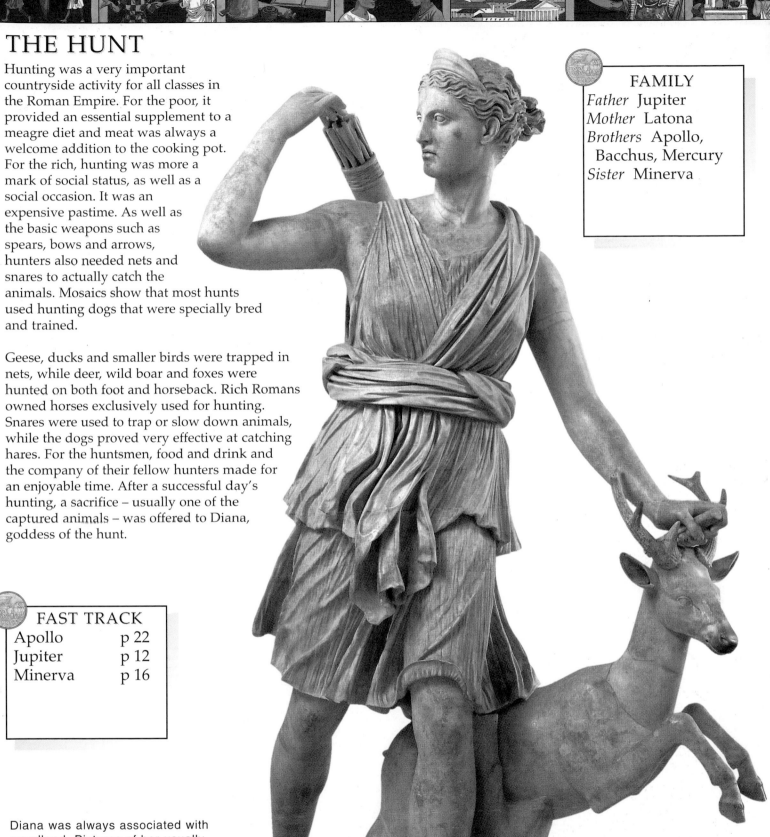

Diana was always associated with woodland. Pictures of her usually show her as a keen huntress with a bow and quiver full of arrows, and she is often accompanied by a stag, as this Roman marble statue (right) shows.

MARS

GOD OF WAR: BATTLES AND WEAPONS

Below is a well-armed and protected Legionary soldier. These were the most highly trained and skilled soldiers in the army. His armour is specially designed to give him both protection and movement.

Spear

Sword

Dagger

Mars, the god of agriculture and war, was very important to the Romans. His main festival time was at the beginning of spring, when plant life was reborn and armies got ready for a new season's fighting. The month of March was named after him. On the 1st of the month troops slaughtered a bull in his honour. The 14th was his feast day, marked by horse races on the Fields of Mars to the north of the city of Rome.

Above is a Roman bronze statue of Mars from the 2nd century AD. Strong, well-armed and aggressive, Mars was the hero of the troops.

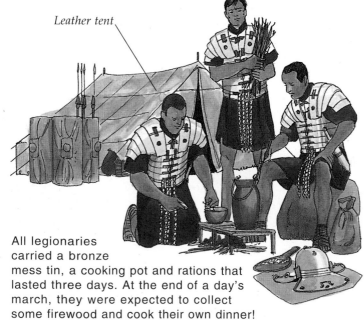

Leather tent

All legionaries carried a bronze mess tin, a cooking pot and rations that lasted three days. At the end of a day's march, they were expected to collect some firewood and cook their own dinner!

Shield

INSIDE STORY

Mars had a soft spot for Venus, the goddess of love, even though she was married to Vulcan – the god of fire and blacksmith to the gods. Vulcan pretended to go away, but had a bronze net, so thin it could not be seen, put around his house. When Mars came to visit Venus, they were both caught in it and their embarrassment was seen by all the gods!

ARMY CAMP

It is not surprising that the army thought so highly of Mars. For long periods Rome was at war – constantly expanding its Empire and then defending it. The army had to be well organised to take and hold so much land.

During campaigns they set up temporary camps that would protect them. First a rectangular ditch and bank was dug with four protected entrances. Then the leather tents were put up and sentries posted to watch for enemy action.

PLUTO

GOD OF THE UNDERWORLD: DEATH AND FUNERALS

After their funeral, the bodies of rich people would be placed in large rectangular or circular tombs called *mausolea* (above). These were designed to impress the living long after the occupant's death. Intricately painted inside, they could be visited by the dead person's family.

Pluto was also known as Dis in Roman times, and he was the god of the dead and the underworld. He was treated with great respect and he could be called upon by striking the earth with a hand. If an animal was to be sacrificed to him, a black sheep was always chosen and the person performing the sacrifice had to look away. Pluto was not actually worshipped and this is why there are very few statues to him.

Cremations took place on a funeral pyre in a special part of the cemetery. Afterwards, the remains were placed in a container or urn (above), usually made of glass, pottery or metal.

INSIDE STORY

A dead person was escorted to the underworld by Mercury. He left them at the River Styx which had to be crossed. A coin – usually put in the corpse's mouth – paid Cheron, the ferryman, to take the dead person across. Cereberus, Pluto's fierce 3-headed dog waited for them at the other side. Three cakes (put in the hands of the corpse) kept him quiet as the dead walked past into the underworld.

This fresco (above) from the 1st century shows a ritual dance that would have taken place at a funeral. Sometimes the dancers acted out mimes and dressed up as ancestors of the dead person. They wore masks, which were called *imagines*.

THE FUNERAL

Wealthy people's funerals were often very elaborate affairs involving professional undertakers who provided mourners, musicians and dancers. The procession would pass all the public places, going through the main streets and stopping in the *forum*. If the deceased was well-known, a speech would be made praising his memory. The procession would pass through the city gates and out along the road to the necropolis. Funerals of the poor took a shorter, direct route to the cemetery and usually involved a cremation. Funeral clubs could be paid into and they would look after the expenses of the deceased's family.

At the burial or cremation site, the mourners usually had a feast in honour of the dead person, as this stone relief (above) shows. Food and drink would be placed in the grave or mausoleum. After nine days of mourning, another feast took place and the dead were also remembered during festivals and anniversaries.

FAMILY
Father Saturn
Brothers Jupiter, Neptune
Sisters Ceres, Juno, Vesta

FESTIVALS
AND CELEBRATIONS

Animals sacrificed to the gods had to be certain colours – white for Jupiter and Juno, and a darker colour for Pluto.

The Romans had a full religious calendar and honoured many gods and goddesses in different festivals throughout the year. Many were originally agricultural festivals, reflecting a time when Romans had had to grow their own corn rather than have other people supply it for them. A festival was a time for visiting the temples of certain gods and making sacrifices to them. If the festivals were not celebrated, the people feared that the gods might turn their backs on Rome and refuse to help!

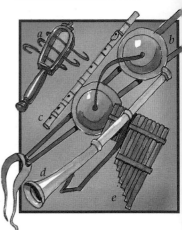

Instruments (above) were often played at religious ceremonies to drown out any sounds that might bring bad luck. They included a type of rattle called a *sistrum* (a), cymbals (b), flutes (c), horns (d) and reed pipes (e).

INSIDE STORY

The most famous of all the festivals was the Lupercalia. On 15th February, at a small cave on the Pallantine Hill called the Lupercal – supposedly the cave where Romulus and Remus had been nursed by the wolf – two teams of young men met. Here they sacrificed goats and a dog and then ate a huge feast. Afterwards, the two teams appeared dressed up in the skins of the recently killed goats and ran a race below the hill. During the race, they whipped the crowd with strips of goats' skin causing great excitement.

Bacchus was the god of wine and he was worshipped in many villas and villages after the grapes had been harvested during October. This was a time of great merriment! As the Empire grew, so too did the taste for wine and it was exported all around the Mediterranean and the far-flung parts of the Empire. Wine from Gaul and Germany was even shipped to Britain. This silver platter (left) from the 4th century AD shows worshippers of Bacchus dancing.

These people (above) are celebrating the Saturnalia festival. This was one of the most important festivals and it happened in mid-winter. It honoured Saturn, the god of seed-sowing. The festival began at his temple with a sacrifice, which was followed by a public feast that all could attend. Shops and businesses closed and everyone had a holiday. The celebrations ran from 17-23rd December. In wealthy houses, slaves were given time off and some were even served by their masters. A 'mock king' was elected who ordered people to do foolish things.

Some festivals were celebrated privately in the home. The Penates, who watched over the larder or food store, were very important household gods. It was essential to please the Penates so that the family had enough food to eat each day. Offerings were made at the house shrine and family and friends were invited to a special meal (left).

GLADIATORS AND CHARIOT RACING

Crowds loved the cut and thrust of the gladiator duels in the arena (above). The word 'arena' comes from the Latin for sand, which was needed to soak up the spilt blood!

INSIDE STORY

The people who fought in the arena were either condemned prisoners, slaves, prisoners of war, criminals or tough professional gladiators. Professional gladiators were trained in special schools called *familiae*. Some were the 'superstars' of their day and had many adoring fans.

The Games (called *ludi*) were originally held as a votive offering to Jupiter. By the time of the Empire, the Emperors realised that they had to pay to put the games on in order to keep the whole population happy. The games always followed a set timetable. After a public banquet the evening before, involving all the contestants, they started off in a procession headed by trumpets and horns to the amphitheatre. This is where the Games took place.

FAST TRACK

Jupiter   p 12

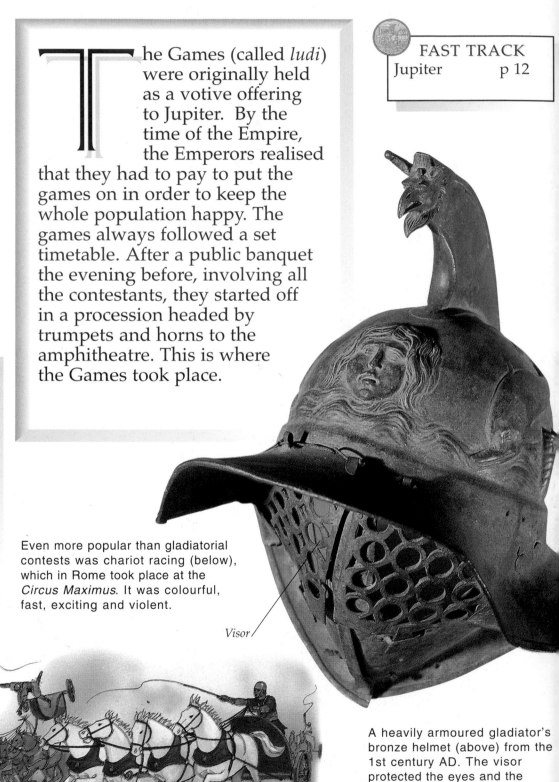

Even more popular than gladiatorial contests was chariot racing (below), which in Rome took place at the *Circus Maximus*. It was colourful, fast, exciting and violent.

Visor

A heavily armoured gladiator's bronze helmet (above) from the 1st century AD. The visor protected the eyes and the guard at the back protected the neck and shoulders.

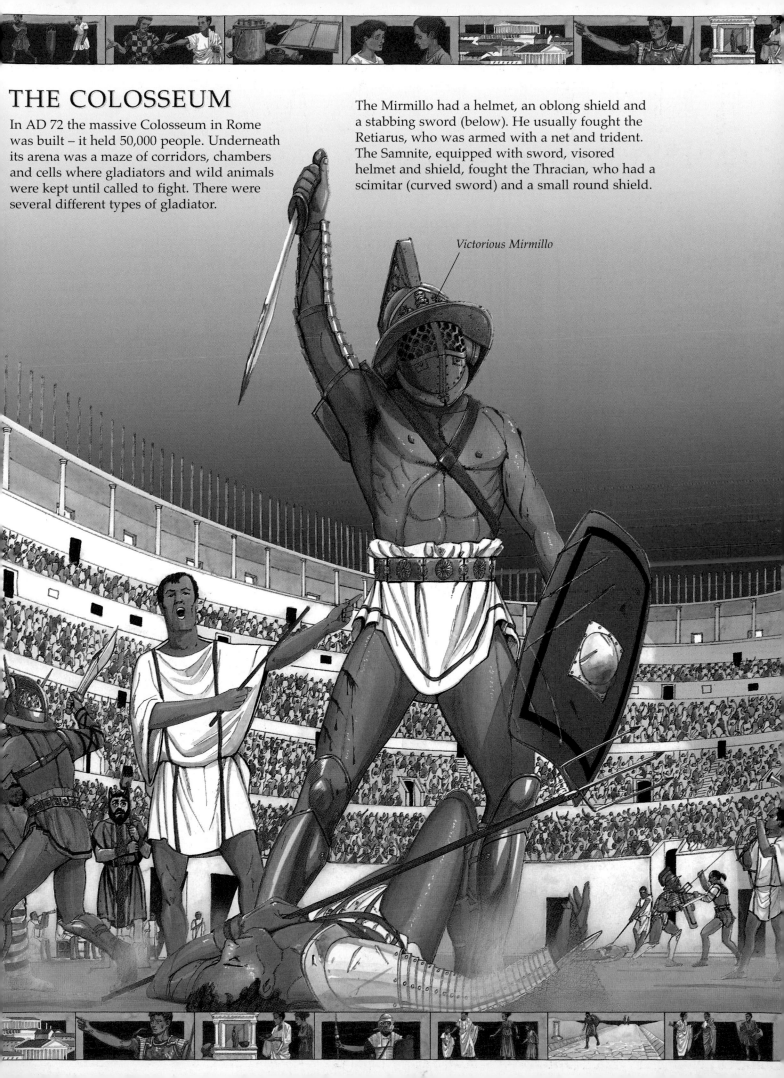

THE COLOSSEUM

In AD 72 the massive Colosseum in Rome was built – it held 50,000 people. Underneath its arena was a maze of corridors, chambers and cells where gladiators and wild animals were kept until called to fight. There were several different types of gladiator.

The Mirmillo had a helmet, an oblong shield and a stabbing sword (below). He usually fought the Retiarus, who was armed with a net and trident. The Samnite, equipped with sword, visored helmet and shield, fought the Thracian, who had a scimitar (curved sword) and a small round shield.

Victorious Mirmillo

DEITIES

AND LOCAL GODS

Fortuna was a Roman deity believed to be the bringer of luck and prosperity. She often carried a *cornucopia*, or 'horn of plenty', which symbolised abundance. It is therefore appropriate that she adorns this public fountain (above), in the Street of Abundance in Pompeii.

In the hot and sunny climate of Italy, a freshwater spring or cool glade of trees were thought to be sacred places where the spirits lived. These were the 'deities' or local gods. They could live anywhere – in rivers, streams, caves, valleys and hills. They did not always have names. A Roman officer stationed in Britain near to Hadrian's Wall set up an altar 'to the gods who inhabit this place'. It was thought far better to do this than to risk naming the wrong god!

Local gods were often concerned with fertility. It was essential that babies were born healthy and survived, and that food was plentiful. These two female deities (above) clearly show these two important functions.

When the Romans reached Bath in England, they found a natural hot-water spa, believed to be inhabited by the Celtic god Sulis. Cleverly, the Romans joined this with Minerva to form the deity Sulis-Minerva. They then proceeded to build a wonderful temple-bath complex using the naturally hot waters, as shown in this picture below.

INSIDE STORY

Many people used local gods to help them curse their enemies or people who had harmed them. They took a slate or tablet and scratched the curse onto it. It would then be nailed on a tree in a grove, or thrown into a stream or pool near to the deity. One such curse read, 'May he who carried off Vilbia from me become as liquid as water... and be struck dumb'.

ROMAN BATHS

There was no particular god of Roman baths, but local deities made their homes in springs and, for this reason, many bath houses had shrines to them. How did the baths work? First you undressed in the changing room and, wearing wooden sandals to protect your feet from the hot floor, you entered the *tepidarium* or warm room. Next you went into the *caldarium* where you would sweat heavily. After a massage with oil, a slave would scrape sweat and dirt off you with a curved blunt knife called a *strigil*. You then took a hot or cold plunge bath.

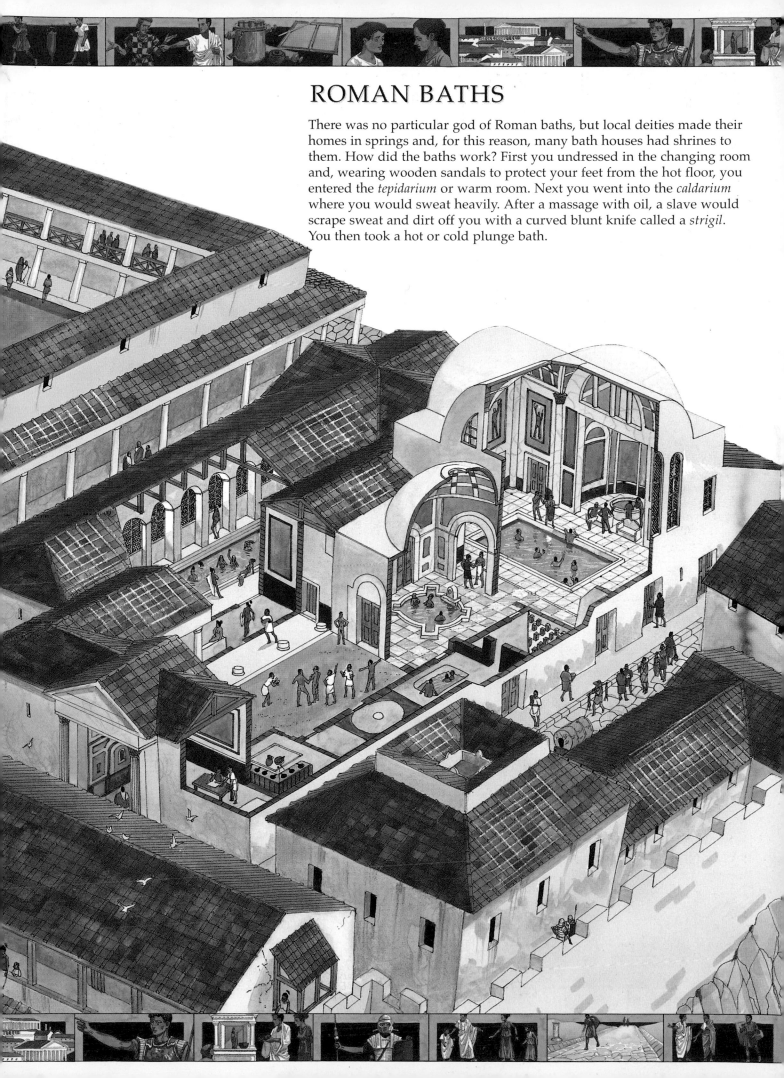

JUDAISM
AND THE TEMPLE AT JERUSALEM

The Jews did not celebrate any of the Roman festivals because they had their own regular 'day of rest' – the Sabbath. The *Menorah* (above), the seven branched candlestick, was lit in the temple on this day.

Of all the religions in the ancient world, Judaism was unusual. It only permitted belief in, and worship of, one god. To worship any other god was forbidden. For the Romans, who added Palestine to the Roman Empire in 63 BC, this caused a problem – they expected subjects within the Empire to worship the Emperor as well as any other gods. However, the Jews had been allies of the Romans since the 2nd century BC and so they were allowed to follow their own religion.

Menorah

In AD 66 the Jews rebelled against Roman rule. For the Romans this was unacceptable and they always crushed rebellions with savage force. The Emperor Titus (son of Vespasian) crushed the revolt in AD 70, destroying Jerusalem and its splendid Temple (see opposite page). After a successful campaign, the army always led a procession, called a Triumph, through Rome. This stone relief carving from a triumphal arch (left) shows the Roman army displaying all the captured booty from Jerusalem, including the *Menorah*.

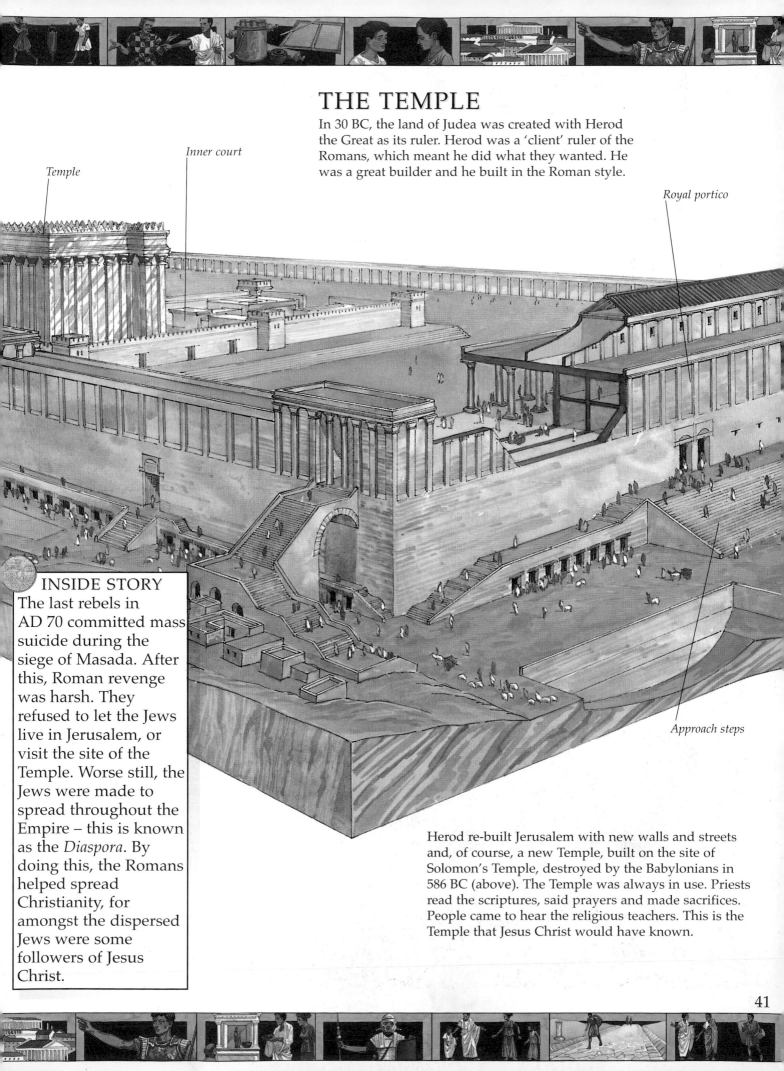

THE TEMPLE

In 30 BC, the land of Judea was created with Herod the Great as its ruler. Herod was a 'client' ruler of the Romans, which meant he did what they wanted. He was a great builder and he built in the Roman style.

Temple

Inner court

Royal portico

Approach steps

INSIDE STORY

The last rebels in AD 70 committed mass suicide during the siege of Masada. After this, Roman revenge was harsh. They refused to let the Jews live in Jerusalem, or visit the site of the Temple. Worse still, the Jews were made to spread throughout the Empire – this is known as the *Diaspora*. By doing this, the Romans helped spread Christianity, for amongst the dispersed Jews were some followers of Jesus Christ.

Herod re-built Jerusalem with new walls and streets and, of course, a new Temple, built on the site of Solomon's Temple, destroyed by the Babylonians in 586 BC (above). The Temple was always in use. Priests read the scriptures, said prayers and made sacrifices. People came to hear the religious teachers. This is the Temple that Jesus Christ would have known.

AND THE CONVERSION OF ANCIENT ROME

Above is the head from a massive bronze statue of Emperor Constantine. The turning point in Constantine's religious belief came in AD 312 when he fought the battle of the Milvian Bridge against his rival Maxentius. Before the battle, he had a vision of the Cross and his troops hastily painted the symbol on their shield. Constantine won the battle.

As far as the Roman Empire was concerned, Christianity was a small, if troublesome, Jewish group. The problem was made worse by the fact that many Jews had been dispersed throughout the Empire and missionaries were spreading the religion to non-Jews. Problems for the Christians began in the reign of Nero who blamed them for a terrible fire in AD 64 which destroyed half of Rome. Persecutions quickly followed.

INSIDE STORY

The most important event to encourage the acceptance of Christianity by the Roman Empire came in the reign of Constantine. With the Edict of Milan he called for both the old, pagan religion and Christianity to live side-by-side. Constantine himself was baptised on his deathbed. By AD 325 Christianity had become the religion of the Roman Empire. The Emperor Julian tried to restore the pagan religions, but a later Emperor, Theodosius I, banned all pagan temples and shrines.

As Christianity slowly spread throughout the Empire, Christians developed signs that they hoped would give them protection. The symbol behind the figure (thought to be Jesus) on this mosaic (left) is one of these. It has been found on floors and wall-paintings in many villas dating from the 3rd century AD onwards.

Between AD 249 and 251, the Emperor Decius had many hundreds of Christians put to death. The Roman tradition of having criminals ripped to death by wild animals was applied to Christians (left). This method of execution was thought suitable for people who were considered to be a threat to the state.

These massacres of Christians took place in amphitheatres all over the Roman Empire. Christians were killed in Lyon, Carthage and, of course, Rome. So many Christians were killed in the Colosseum (below) that a wooden cross has been erected in their memory.

GLOSSARY

Aqueduct A channel or bridge that carries water.

Archery A sport that involves shooting with bows and arrows.

Atrium An unroofed or part-roofed hall in a Roman house.

Brigands Robbers who roamed the countryside in gangs.

Cella The sacred room of a temple or shrine.

Colonnade A walkway with columns holding up a protective roof.

Commerce All types of business and trade.

Cornucopia The horn of plenty. It represented great abundance.

Cup-bearer A special servant.

Dedicated Devoted to a god or goddess.

Fermented When the sugar in food or liquid has turned into alcohol.

Hides The skins of animals.

Incense A perfume that produces a sweet smell when burnt.

Lyre An ancient stringed instrument with a U-shaped frame.

Menorah A Jewish seven-branched candlestick.

Merchants People engaged in trade – buying and selling.

Necropolis A Roman cemetery.

Oracle An important shrine where the gods were asked for advice or prophecies.

Pagan A person who worships the gods of nature. In ancient Rome, it meant pre-Christian gods.

Pantheon The whole range of gods from one particular time.

Peristyle garden An enclosed garden at the centre of a Roman house, usually surrounded by a colonnade.

Pharmacopia A chemist.

Podium A raised platform.

Portico A small covered area, usually in the garden of a Roman house.

Prophecy A statement that predicts the future.

Prosperous Wealthy, or successful with money.

Sacrifice The slaughter of an animal as an offering to a god.

Sanctuary A sacred space in a temple or theatre, often dedicated to a particular god.

Sarcophagus A stone coffin.

Shrine A special place for worship.

Standard A symbol – perhaps an eagle or wolf – carried on a pole, that identified a particular unit in the Roman army.

Stone-relief A carving or sculpture in the side of a block of stone.

Threshed Corn or wheat that has been beaten to separate the grain from the husk.

Trident A three-pronged fork.

Underworld The place under the earth where the ancient Romans believed the dead lived.

Urn A vase or container made of clay.

Vestal Virgins Six priestesses who tended to the eternal flame in the Temple of Vesta, Rome.

Votive offering An offering made to a god, usually in the hope of a favour in return.

Yoke A wooden bar attached to the neck of an animal to help it pull a vehicle or plough.

INDEX